Trombone Essentials

11 Recital and Contest Solos for Tenor and Bass Trombone

Arranged and Edited by Douglas Yeo

ED 4082

First printing: April 1999

cover illustration: Stölzel, BIST DU BEI MIR,
facsimile of the *Anna Magdalena Bach Notebook* (1725)

ISBN 978-0-7935-9493-1

G. SCHIRMER, Inc.

PREFACE

This collection of trombone solos represents an attempt to provide the serious player with suitable repertoire for recital and contest. Trombonists are confronted with a dilemma when it comes to selecting repertoire preceding the 20th century, as the instrument has only recently attracted composers to write for it in a serious way. While we can thank composers such as Albrechtsberger and Wagenseil for their fine solo contributions for alto trombone, such works remain out of the practical range of most players unless transcribed into lower keys (as Henry C. Smith did with the Wagenseil *Concerto* in his *First Solos for the Trombone Player*).

Music of the Baroque and Classical periods offers trombonists much to explore and develop—it calls for a nimble technique, a lyrical style and an important sense of rhythmic emphasis. For many years, trombonists have borrowed pieces originally written for flute, cello, bassoon and voice, and made them their own. Here in this collection are complete works transcribed specifically for trombone and piano, along with some selected unaccompanied works that work splendidly on trombone.

I have selected eleven works that I and many of my students have used successfully in concert. All but one are playable on tenor and bass trombone; the Schumann *Adagio and Allegro* has been included especially for the bass trombonist. The selections cover a wide range of musical styles and time periods. My primary goal has been to edit the works in a way that reflects appropriate performance practice of the period and at the same time ensures an idiomatic style for the trombone.

The words below serve as only the briefest of introductions to each work. I hope that trombonists, after being inspired by the fine music represented in this book, will further explore the life and music of each composer.

—DOUGLAS YEO
Bass Trombonist, Boston Symphony Orchestra

Benedetto Marcello (1686–1739) is familiar to trombonists for his many solo sonatas for various instruments. The *Sonata No. 1* in F major is the first in a series of six sonatas Marcello wrote for cello, published in 1732 in Amsterdam as his opus 1. The four-movement structure is typical of many Baroque sonatas, and the transcription from cello to trombone is a natural one. As with most of the Baroque selections in this book, the original manuscript contains few dynamic or phrase markings. I have tried to create a useful performing edition for trombone while taking into account performance practice of the time as outlined in the three great Baroque treatises on the subject: Quantz's *On Playing the Flute* (1752), C.P.E. Bach's *Essay on the True Art of Playing Keyboard Instruments* (1753), and Geminiani's *The Art of Playing on the Violin* (1751). A light touch in the fast movements coupled with an appropriate sense of the strong (1 & 3) and weak (2 & 4) beats will help maintain forward motion and liveliness.

Wolfgang Amadeus Mozart (1756–1791) wrote many operas, some of which feature significant parts for trombone—including *The Magic Flute*, the next to last opera he completed before his death. It contains this beautiful aria sung by the high priest Sarastro about the young couple Tamino and Pamina, who are about to be put through difficult tasks. The text demands a noble and reverent style from the soloist.

O Isis und Osiris, schenket der Weisheit
Geist dem neuen Paar!
Die ihr der Wandrer Schritte lenket, stärkt
mit Geduld sie in Gefahr.
Laßt sie der Prüfung Früchte sehen, doch
sollen sie zu Grabe gehen,
so lohnt der Tugend kühnen Lauf, nehmt sie
in euren Wohnsitz auf.

O Isis and Osiris, endow the new couple with
the spirit of wisdom!
Strengthen them, whose wanderers' feet you
guide, with patience in perilous situations!
Let them see the fruits of their trial. Yet,
should they die,
reward virtue's daring endeavor and take
them into your dwelling place.

(TRANSLATION: HOWARD WEINER)

Georg Philipp Telemann (1681–1767) is represented by two works in this collection. His *Six Canonic Sonatas* (*Sei duetti*) for two flutes are miniature masterpieces of the canonic form. Since both players play exactly the same music (separated by one or two measures as indicated on the part), the second player can either exactly imitate or creatively ornament what has gone before. Telemann's mastery is especially evident in the third movement of No. 3, where he begins in C minor, modulates to C major and then returns to C minor, all the while keeping both parts in perfect harmonic unity. Telemann's *Twelve Fantasies* for unaccompanied flute, written in 1732–33, provide the trombonist with many rewarding challenges. Experiment with alternative slide positions in order to have the smoothest flow in the fast movements, and try taking frequent, small breaths (you may wish to try quick "sniff breaths" through your nose while keeping the mouthpiece on your embouchure) so as to not upset the forward motion of the piece.

The beautiful aria *Bist du bei mir* ("If you are with me," or as it is more popularly known, "If thou be near") was thought for many years to have come from the pen of Johann Sebastian Bach (1685–1750). It appears in the notebook he gave in 1725 to his second wife, Anna Magdalena, which also contains many famous short clavier pieces, arias and more substantial keyboard works. Recent scholarship has determined that most of the material in the notebook is not by Bach after all, and that *Bist du bei mir* was in fact written by **Gottfried Heinrich Stölzel** (1690–1749), a highly respected German composer of Bach's day. Despite his massive output, this aria (originally for soprano and strings) is Stölzel's primary legacy to our time. It has been set to many texts over the years, both sacred and secular; here is Stölzel's original text, along with a literal English translation:

Bist du bei mir, geh ich mit Freuden zum
Sterben und zu meiner Ruh,
zum Sterben und zu meiner Ruh.
Ach, wie vergnügt wär so mein Ende,
es drückten deine schönen Hände getreuen
Augen zu.

If you are with me, I go gladly to meet death
and to my rest,
to meet death and to my rest.
Oh, how delightful my end would be,
if it were your lovely hands that closed my
faithful eyes.

(TRANSLATION: HOWARD WEINER)

Johann Sebastian Bach (1685–1750) is considered one of the pillars of western music. His musical output consisted of hundreds of works, including over 300 church cantatas and of course his *Suites* for solo cello, which are frequently played by trombonists. His *Magnificat* (1723) tells the Biblical story of Luke 1:46-55. *Quia fecit mihi magna* (originally in A major) is the fifth of the *Magnificat*'s twelve movements, and was originally for bass solo with orchestra.

Quia fecit mihi magna qui potens est, et
sanctum nomen ejus.
He that is mighty has done great things for
me, and holy is His name.

Jules Massenet (1842–1912) is remembered primarily as a composer of *bel canto* opera. *Thaïs*, composed in 1894, is a tale of love, faith and redemption in ancient Egypt. The famous *Meditation*, originally scored for solo violin and orchestra, provides a moment of reflection for the audience between scenes one and two of Act II as the principal female character in the opera, Thaïs, realizes that her life is in need of the kind of change that spiritual regeneration alone can provide. It is a moment of intense self-realization and emotion. This transcription can be played successfully with either piano or organ accompaniment.

Nikolai Rimsky-Korsakov (1844–1908) is well known to trombonists for his *Trombone Concerto* (1877), composed just before his *Concertstück for Clarinet and Military Band* (1878). The Andante of the *Concertstück* provides a gentle relief from the technical demands of the outer movements of the work and contains echoes of the middle movement of the *Trombone Concerto*.

The *Adagio and Allegro* of **Robert Schumann** (1810–1856) was written for horn and piano in a period of four days in 1849; Schumann's original title for the work was *Romanze und Allegro*. It is a virtuoso composition for horn from a composer who knew well what the instrument could accomplish. While Schumann wrote no solo music for trombone, his *Adagio and Allegro* has long been popular with bass trombonists and tubists who can exploit the technical and musical demands of the piece. Courageous tenor trombonists might wish to tackle the piece an octave higher than notated, a feat perhaps better suited for alto trombone.

Carl Philipp Emanuel Bach (1714–1788) was the second surviving son of J.S. Bach and his first wife, Maria Barbara. His *Sonata* for unaccompanied flute was written in 1747; the original manuscript has been lost but the first edition of 1763, published in Berlin, survives. I have chosen to order the movements in a sensible Allegro(1)–Poco Adagio–Allegro(2) format, although the first edition, perhaps erroneously or because a fourth movement is missing, has them ordered Poco Adagio–Allegro(1)–Allegro(2). Whenever possible I have maintained Bach's original phrasing while making trills and other ornamentation more trombonistic.

Après un rêve ("After a Dream"), by **Gabriel Fauré** (1845–1924), is one of the most famous songs ever written, owing much of its popularity to the transcription for cello by Pablo Casals. The insistent piano accompaniment provides a contrast to the flowing solo line. It was published as Fauré's opus 7 no. 1, to an anonymous text rendered in French by Romain Bussine.

Dans un sommeil, que charmait ton image,
je revais le bonheur... ardent mirage;
Tes yeux étaient plus doux, ta voix pure et sonore,
Tu rayonnais comme un ciel éclairé par l'aurore;
Tu m'appelais et je quittais la terre pour m'enfuir avec toi vers la lumiére;
Les cieux pour nous entr'ouvraient leurs nues,
Splendeurs inconnues, lueurs divines entrevues.
Hélas! Hélas, triste réveil des songes,
Je t'appelle, o nuit, rends-moi tes mensonges,
Reviens, reviens radieuse, reviens, o nuit mystérieuse!

In a sleep which was enchanted by your image, I was dreaming happiness... burning illusion;
Your eyes were gentler, your voice pure and resounding,
You shone like a sky lit up by the dawn,
You were calling me and I was leaving the earth to flee with you towards the light;
The skies for us parted their clouds,
Unknown splendors, glimpses of divine rays of light.
Alas! Alas, sad awakening from dreams,
I'm calling you, oh night, give me back your lies,
Come back, come back radiant, come back, oh mysterious night!

(TRANSLATION: KAREN DAY GIRONDEL)

SONATA No. 1

from *Six Sonatas for Cello*

Benedetto Marcello
arranged by Douglas Yeo

I

II

Allegro (♩ = 100)

13
f
p
f
p
16
mp
mp
19
mf
mf
22
p
p

25
f
p
f
p
28
f
f
31
p
p
34

III

IV

24
f
f
30
p
p
tr
tr
tr
35
cresc.
40
f
f

O ISIS UND OSIRIS

Aria from *The Magic Flute*, K 620

Wolfgang Amadeus Mozart

arranged by Douglas Yeo

28
mf
35
mp
mf
42
f
mf dim.
mp
49
p

BIST DU BEI MIR

Aria from the *Anna Magdalena Bach Notebook*, 1725

Gottfried Heinrich Stölzel
previously attributed to J.S. Bach
arranged by Douglas Yeo

Andante (♩ = 72)

poco rall.

QUIA FECIT MIHI MAGNA

Aria from *Magnificat*, BWV 243

Johann Sebastian Bach
arranged by Douglas Yeo

10
poco cresc.
poco cresc.
13
mf
mf
16
dim.
mp
mp
mf
mf
19

22
tr
f
p
25
p
cresc.
cresc.
28
f
f
31

MEDITATION
from *Thaïs*

Jules Massenet
arranged by Douglas Yeo

15
f
f
p
f
f
20
rall.
a tempo
più mosso
p
p
mf
mf
più f
25
f
f
p sub.
p
30
f molto appassionato
cresc.

34
più mosso agitato
più f
sf
sf
sf
38
rall.
a tempo
pp
sff
dolce
43
rall.
p
f
48
a tempo
p sub.
pp
f

52
ff
f
f
p
f
57
rall.
a tempo
p
f
pp
mf
f
61
p
p
f
66
mf
p
calmato
f
p
calmato
dim.
ppp

Trombone Essentials

11 Recital and Contest Solos for Tenor and Bass Trombone

Arranged and Edited by Douglas Yeo

TROMBONE

ED 4082

First printing: April 1999

ISBN 978-0-7935-9493-1

G. SCHIRMER, *Inc.*

Trombone

SONATA No. 1

from *Six Sonatas for Cello*

Benedetto Marcello
arranged by Douglas Yeo

I

II

13
f
p
16
mp
19
mf
22
p
25
f
p
28
f
31
p
34

III

Largo (♩ = 56)

IV

Allegro (♩ = 108)

O ISIS UND OSIRIS

Aria from *The Magic Flute*, K 620

Wolfgang Amadeus Mozart
arranged by Douglas Yeo

2 Trombones *

CANONIC SONATA NO. 3
from *Six Sonatas (Sei duetti)*

Georg Philipp Telemann
arranged by Douglas Yeo

I

* Second trombone begins at 𝄋 and ends at the fermata.

30
33
37
40
II
Soave (gentle, sweet) ♩. = 44
p
4
6
9
p
f
12
15

III

Allegro assai (♩. = 64)

mf

11

22

32

42

52

mp espressivo

63

73

mf

83

95

107

119

129

BIST DU BEI MIR

Aria from the *Anna Magdalena Bach Notebook*, 1725

Gottfried Heinrich Stölzel
previously attributed to J.S. Bach
arranged by Douglas Yeo

QUIA FECIT MIHI MAGNA

Aria from *Magnificat*, BWV 243

Johann Sebastian Bach
arranged by Douglas Yeo

Andante con moto (♩ = 84)

5 2
p dolce *mf*

MEDITATION

from *Thaïs*

Jules Massenet
arranged by Douglas Yeo

Andante religioso

2 3 5
p

7 *rall.* , *a tempo* 3
p *p sub.*

12 3 3 3 3
f

17
rall.
a tempo
f
p
22
più mosso
mf
f
27
p sub.
32
più mosso agitato
f molto appassionato
36
rall.
40
a tempo
pp
45
rall.
a tempo
p
p sub.
50
ff
54
rall.
a tempo
f
p
60
f
p
66
mf
p
calmato

ANDANTE
from *Concertstück for Clarinet and Military Band*

Nikolai Rimsky-Korsakov
arranged by Douglas Yeo

ADAGIO AND ALLEGRO

Op. 70

Robert Schumann
arranged by Douglas Yeo

Allegro con brio (♩ = 144)
62
f
66
sf
sf
71
cresc.
ff
75
sf
p
81
2
p
p
88
cresc.
93
p
fp
99
f
f
104
sf
109
sf
cresc.
114
ff
118
Poco tranquillo
sf
p
124
cresc.
p
131
cresc.
137
cresc.
cresc.

Tempo I
Più mosso

Trombone
(unaccompanied)

SONATA
in C minor, Wq 132
(originally in A minor)

I

Carl Philipp Emanuel Bach
arranged by Douglas Yeo

61
p
67
cresc. poco a poco
mf
74
p
80
86
91
poco rit.
a tempo
f
mf
97
f
p
f
103
p
f
p
109
f
115

II

47
p
mf p
53
mp
58
p
63
mf
mf p
69
mf p
mf
75
80
3
p
86
mf pp
f
p

III

Allegro (♩. = 66)
mf
9
16
23
f
31
p
mp
39
f
p
f
p
f
46
3
mp
f
53
f
p
61
mf
p
mf
68
mp
p
mp
p
mp
p
mp
p

77
mp
84
91
mp
cresc.
99
mf
107
115
121
mf
cresc.
128
3
f
mf p
mp p
mp p
136
cresc.
rit.
f
143
3
a tempo
mp cresc.
rit.

Trombone
(unaccompanied)

FANTAISIE NO. 2
in C minor, TWV 40:3
(originally in A minor)

Georg Philipp Telemann
arranged by Douglas Yeo

I

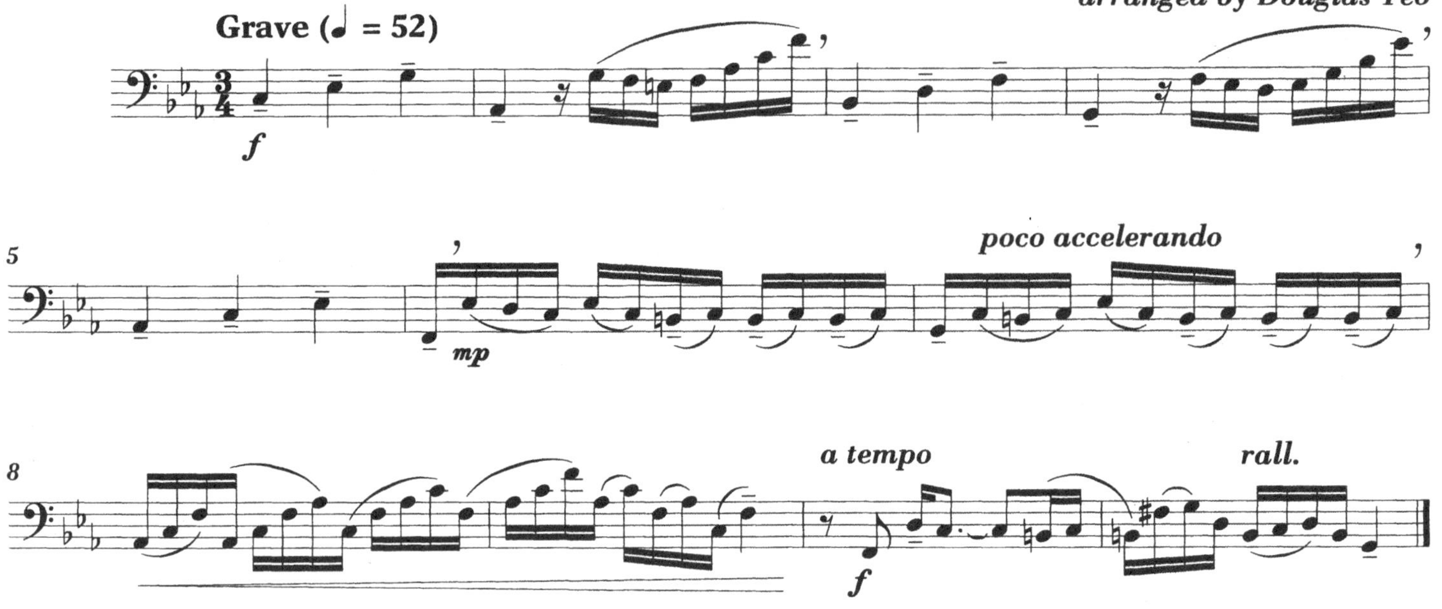

Grave (♩ = 52)

f

5 *mp* *poco accelerando*

8 *a tempo* *f* *rall.*

II

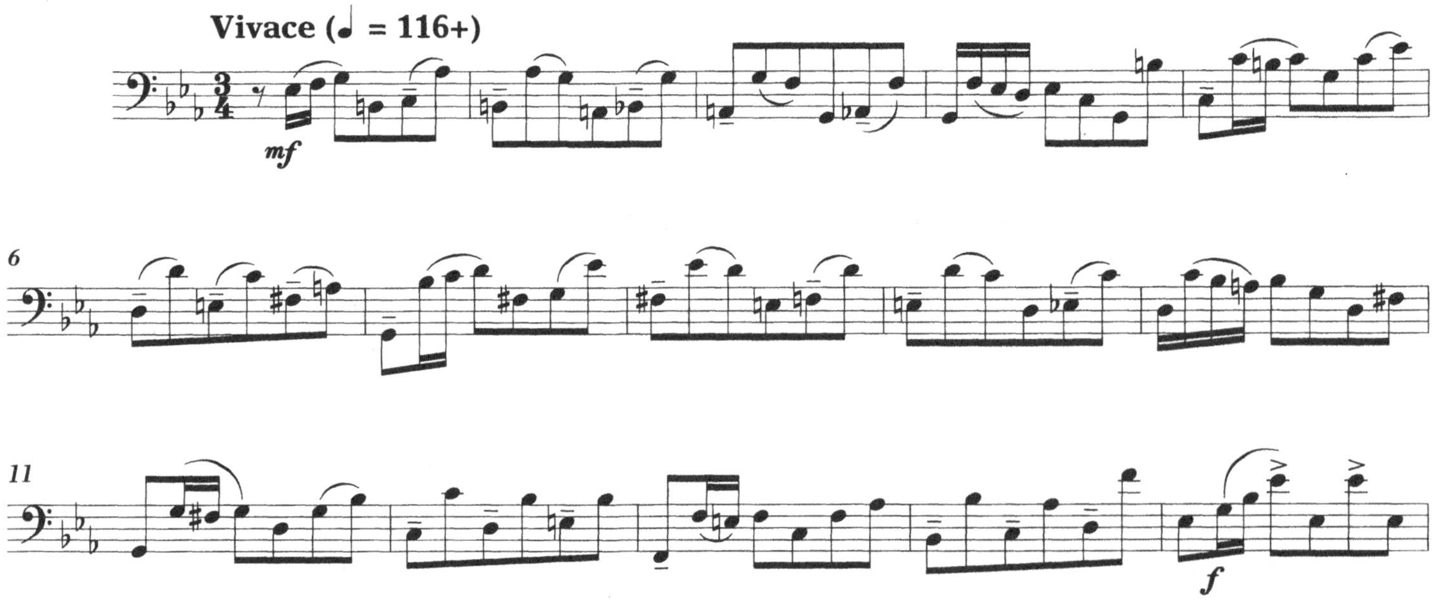

Vivace (♩ = 116+)

mf

16
p
f
6
1
20
rit.
a tempo
mf
25
f
p
mf
30
(𝄾)
f
p
35
f
(𝄾)
40
p
f
45
6
1
p
6
1
rall.
f

III
Adagio (♪ = 64)
mp
cresc. poco a poco
f
p
rall.
IV
Allegro (♩ = 112+)
f
mf
p
(f)
cresc. poco a poco
mf cresc. poco a poco
rit. (2nd time)

APRÈS UN RÊVE

Gabriel Fauré

arranged by Douglas Yeo

ANDANTE

from *Concertstück for Clarinet and Military Band*

Nikolai Rimsky-Korsakov
arranged by Douglas Yeo

Andante (♩ = 72)

Più mosso
rall.
Tempo I

29
32
35
rall.
38
p

ADAGIO AND ALLEGRO

Op. 70

Robert Schumann
arranged by Douglas Yeo

19
p
p
cresc.
24
p sub.
p
28
sf
sf
fp
fp
f
sf
32
sf
f
sfp
f
p cresc.

37
f
dim.
f
dim.
cresc.
Ped.
44
p
f
p
Ped.
51
Ped.
56
pp
pp
dim.
pp
Ped.
Ped.
attacca

Allegro con brio (♩ = 144)
62
f
f
Ped.
66
sf
sf
69
sf
sf
72
cresc.
cresc.
ff
ff
Ped.

75
78
81
84
sf
p
fp
cresc.

87
p
cresc.
p
cresc.
Ped.
*
Ped.
90
*
93
p
fp
96

99
f
f
102
f
f
Ped.
✻
105
sf
Ped. ✻
Ped. ✻
Ped.
✻
108
sf

111
sf
cresc.
sf
cresc.
114
ff
ff
Ped.
*
117
sf
sf
sf
Ped.
* Ped.
* Ped.
*
Ped.
*
120
Poco tranquillo
p
p
124
cresc.
cresc.

128
dim.
p
p
132
cresc.
cresc.
136
cresc.
cresc.
139
cresc.
cresc.
Ped.
Ped.
143
Tempo I
f
f
Ped.
Ped.

147
f
Ped. *
Ped. *
Ped.
*
151
sf
sf
154
sf
sf
157
cresc.
cresc.
ff
ff
Ped.
*

160
sf
Ped.
163
sf
p
166
169
fp
cresc.
p

172
p
cresc.
p
3
Ped.
*
cresc.
Ped.
175
*
178
p
fp
181

184
f
f
187
f
f
Ped.
*
190
sf
Ped. *
Ped. *
Ped.
*
193
sf
cresc.
cresc.

196
sf
sf
3
sf
199
sf
sf
sf
202
sf
sf
205
sf
ff
ff
sf
sf

Più mosso

APRÈS UN RÊVE

Op. 7, No. 1

Gabriel Fauré

arranged by Douglas Yeo

17
p
21
25
cresc. poco a poco
cresc. poco a poco
29
f
f

33
mf
mf
37
cresc.
cresc.
41
f
p
mf
p
45
pp
pp